Faith in His Future

Adele Pilkington

Faith in His Future

Onwards and Upwards Publishers

Berkeley House, 11 Nightingale Crescent, Leatherhead, Surrey, KT24 6PD.

www.onwardsandupwards.org

Printed in the UK.

ISBN: 978-1-907509-89-6

Graphic design: Leah-Maarit

Endorsements

Adele Pilkington's book includes a delightful collection of creative poetry, inspired by the many men and women of faith in the Old Testament referred to in the book of Hebrews. This is an inspirational reflection on how we all need faith to believe that God has a purpose for our lives, however insignificant we deem them to be. It is beautifully illustrated with memorable poems, describing Bible verses which we might know but fail to apply to ourselves.

Fiona Castle OBE
International Christian Speaker and Author

There is a simplicity about these poems that is rather deceptive. Read each one with the relevant biblical story to hand and you find they do more than re-tell the story surrounding each character; they illuminate it in a way that is relevant and applicable to the life of faith today.

Revd Dr Sandy Roger
Former Principal of Faith Mission Bible College
Minister at Coatbridge Middle Church

These poems bring a refreshing and uplifting light to familiar and well-loved Bible stories. Looking beyond the basic narrative, they draw the reader in to reflect upon the individuals at the heart of each account and challenge us as we read how they lived out their faith.

Valerie Sim
Local Schools Worker, Scripture Union Scotland

This book is dedicated to all those
who have lived lives faithful to God
despite the consequences: those who
are well-known and those known
only to God; those who have already
reached their eternal home and those
who are still "looking forward to the
city with foundations, whose
architect and builder is God."
(Hebrews 11:1)

Contents

www.**adelepoems**.co.uk

Prologue

This collection of verses is based on Hebrews chapter 11, a part of the *Bible* which explores the lives of faith of a number of individuals from differing backgrounds. Whilst the word faith can have different meanings to different people, in the context of this Bible passage it means 'a confident hope'.

Hebrews 11:1

Now faith is confidence in what we hope for and assurance about what we do not see.

Faith is a precious gift from God and is part of His saving work in our lives. By taking hold of this gift and using it daily in our lives, we are enabled to grow to become more like His Son, Jesus, our Lord and Saviour, the author and perfecter of our faith. By this means we are enabled to live the lives God has called us to live.

The passage in Hebrews 11 is often called faith's 'hall of fame' and the individuals detailed within the passage are called 'heroes of faith'. When we explore the lives of each of the individuals named in this Bible passage, these might seem unlikely titles. None would be more surprised by these titles than the individuals themselves, as they would have considered their lives ordinary and were well aware of their own human faults and failings. However, each of their lives demonstrate what can be achieved by placing faith in the one Creator God, who designed and oversees every aspect of the universe in which we live, who is unchanging, eternal and always faithful.

The plans which God has for establishing His promised future kingdom of peace and justice have always depended upon the outworking of faith in the lives of individuals. The majority of the individuals highlighted in the following pages did not see their faith realised in their own life time, as most of them died before the birth of Jesus Christ. However, they looked forward to His eternal kingdom and to the fulfilment of all God's promises.

Hebrews 11:15-6

If they had been thinking of the country they had left, they would have had opportunity to return. Instead, they were longing for a better country – a heavenly one. Therefore God is not ashamed to be called their God, for He has prepared a city for them.

The pages of this book record only a few of these ordinary individuals who achieved extraordinary things by placing their trust in God. The Bible, both in Old and New Testament, recounts the lives of many more similar individuals, and history records countless more who have lived and died since Bible times. Their faithfulness is a source of encouragement. In reading of their lives and struggles we can see that we are not alone, and our circumstances are not unique. Like them we need to go on with God, to claim the inheritance which He alone can give. The following verses from Hebrews chapter 12 explain this reality more eloquently than I could ever hope to do.

Hebrews 12:1-2

Therefore, since we are surrounded by such a great cloud of witnesses, let us throw off everything that hinders and the sin that so easily entangles. And let us run with perseverance the race marked out for us, fixing our eyes on Jesus, the author and perfecter of our faith. For the joy set before him He endured the cross, scorning its shame, and sat down at the right hand of the throne of God.

May these verses encourage you in your faith.

Adele Pilkington

SAVING FAITH

Habakkuk 2:4

See, the enemy is puffed up; his desires are not upright —but the righteous person will live by his faithfulness.

Introduction

The stories recorded in Hebrews 11 are mostly of men who had no formal education and who had limited earthly possessions or status. These stories also present very 'human' men, from a 'warts and all' perspective, who struggled as much with themselves as with others. Yet in each case God had a specific plan for them to fulfil, and by faith in Him they were able to overcome their own limitations or the prejudices of others and achieve all that God intended. Though written centuries ago, their lives speak afresh of the struggles we can face in our own lives and show that with God's help we too can be overcomers.

Little is known about some of the men recorded in Hebrews chapter 11, such as Abel or Methuselah, but their deeds are worthy of their account in these Bible verses. Others, such as Noah or Joseph, may be better known. Noah was a man who ignored the scorn and ridicule of his own generation to do what God asked him to do and brought salvation to many of God's creatures. Joseph's life could have been cut short by his own pride, and yet God humbled him before exalting him to a position he could never had dreamed of, and through which he was able to help countless others.

Abraham began a lineage which God had foretold. Despite Abraham's desire to 'run ahead' of God and do things in his own way, God remained faithful to him and made his descendants as numerous as the grains of sand on the seashore:

Hebrews 11:12
And so from this one man, and he as good as dead, came descendants as numerous as the stars in the sky and as countless as the sand on the seashore.

In Isaac's life we see a foreshadowing of the humble sacrifice that God's only Son made to pay the penalty for our sin at Calvary's cross. Initially, Jacob was not a character you would choose as your best friend, having stolen even from his own brother and being known as a deceiver. Yet in his struggle with God, he received a new name and status, and as a beloved child of God was able to do his part in seeing God's promises fulfilled. Moses was, by the outworking of God's plan, born into a life of privilege rather than servitude. However, he turned his back on all that this lifestyle offered in order to save his own people. This was not an easy choice for Moses, and he struggled throughout his life with fear of his own inadequacies. Yet God patiently encouraged and provided for him, to the extent that Moses' faith grew and he enjoyed a closer walk with God than many other humans have known to this day.

Whilst the passage in Hebrews 11 records the deeds of men who lived in Old Testament times, the Bible as a whole records many men who lived lives of faith. The disciples of Jesus and the apostle Paul would surely have been added to faith's 'hall of fame' if the book of Hebrews had been written at a later point in history. In fact, it would take thousands of volumes of text to record the lives of those who have remained faithful to God down the centuries and will reap their promised heavenly reward.

The majority of these individuals will not be well known in human history, as they are likely to have lived seemingly insignificant lives, having enjoyed no earthly power or status. However, each of their lives is known to God and precious to Him. When our earthly span has ended, only that which has been done in service to God will have any everlasting significance. Let us be encouraged, as we go about our daily lives in faithful service to Him, un-noticed by the world, that God sees and will reward those who earnestly seek Him.

Hebrews 11:6

And without faith it is impossible to please God, because anyone who comes to Him must believe that He exists and that He rewards those who earnestly seek Him.

Heroes of the Faith

So many heroes of the faith,
So many tales to tell,
Of Gideon, David, Samson,
Jephthah and Samuel.

So many more who suffered wrongs,
Tortured, friendless, homeless,
Turned despair to advantage,
Though to the world seemed powerless.

What secret of their courage,
Justice, victory from the brink?
Faith in the one true God, who does
More than we can ask or think!

Are these just tales from history,
Of days of valour gone?
Or do they speak of greater things,
God intended for each one?

As we unite our faith with theirs,
We become part of their story;
As God's kingdom comes and will is done,
We will reign with them in glory.

Hebrews 11:32-33a

And what more shall I say? I do not have time to tell about Gideon, Barak, Samson and Jephthah, about David and Samuel and the prophets, who through faith conquered kingdoms, administered justice, and gained what was promised.

Adele Pilkington

A Better Sacrifice

His blood cried out from underground,
He paid the greatest price,
His brother was his murderer,
What cost his sacrifice?

As Abel gently kept his flocks,
His brother tilled hard soil,
Bitterness raging in his heart,
No reward for all his toil?

Cain took his crops, but kept the best,
Thought God would be appeased,
But with his brother's sacrifice
God smiled and was most pleased.

The sin that led to Adam's fall
Reared up once more in Cain,
Abel lifeless in the dust,
By his brother cruelly slain.

God took Abel and gave him rest
From all life's trials and woes;
In God we too can stand each test
As life on earth endures.

Hebrews 11:4

*By faith Abel brought God a better offering than Cain did.
By faith he was commended as righteous, when God spoke
well of his offerings. And by faith Abel still speaks, even
though he is dead.*

For earthly treasures pass away,
Decline and turn to dust,
Whilst heaven's riches brightly shine
For all who in God trust.

Abel's loss was heaven's gain.
Will we too when life is done
Find that greater weight of glory,
Eternal rest, true peace with God?

Walking with God

The father of Methuselah,
Much famed for his longevity;
But of Enoch little known,
A life of relative brevity.

We know he sought to walk in ways
That pleased his God and King,
Walked by faith and not by sight,
Sought a legacy enduring.

No grave to mark his earthly walk,
Yet God's Word records his fame:
God took him and he was no more,
His life wrought eternal gain.

When our earthly span is o'er
As years flash by so fast,
As we reflect on all we've done,
Only that done for Christ will last.

Will we, like Enoch, find our names
In the Lamb's life-book written?
Or as we stand with empty hands
Will we find no hope in heaven?

Hebrews 11:5

By faith Enoch was taken from this life, so that he did not experience death: "He could not be found, because God had taken him away." For before he was taken, he was commended as one who pleased God.

Secure in God's Promises

In a land which knew no rain,
Noah built by God's design
A boat to hold his family,
Animals – two of every kind.
Though many stood and mocked him
Whilst relaxing in the sun,
He continued with his labour,
Until God's work was done.

Sure of the guidance God had given,
Trusting in God's plan,
He gathered loved ones safe inside,
And then the rains began.
The waters rose, the people cried,
No longer jeers but fear,
Life ebbing in the rising flood,
None left to shed a tear.

Genesis 6:9
Noah was a righteous man, blameless among the people of his time, and he walked faithfully with God.

Noah battled with emotions,
Rising, falling, with the spate,
Those who failed to heed his warning,
A watery grave, their hopeless fate.
Forty days of rain relentless,
His family groaned and yearned for land;
Noah's faith remained unflinching,
On God's promise he would stand.

As the clouds and darkness faded,
Sun again lit up the sky;
A raven, then a dove take flight,
Finding safety up on high.
Noah prayed and waited patiently,
Until he stood on solid ground.
'Go forth and fill this land' [1] God said;
Noah's family gathered round.

Noah gave thanks and praise to God,
Who promised He never would
Judge human sin this way again
By destroying the earth with flood.
As a symbol of enduring truth,
God painted in the sky
A many coloured rainbow –
A sign He alone designed.

---

[1] Genesis 9:1

As Noah found God's word is true,
His promise still endures,
Though life's torrents rush around us,
In God's hands we are secure.
Our faith, though like a mustard seed,
When placed in God above,
Means we're safe for all eternity,
Upheld by our Father's love.

A Father of Nations

The father of many nations –
Who would have thought it so? –
The promise God made Abram
In a time so long ago.
Years sped by so fleetingly,
And still he had no son.
He saw his wife through dimming eyes;
Their hope now seemed forlorn.

Yet he knew his God was faithful,
He had proved this to be true;
He would spare this son, provide a ram,
Sacrifice for honour due.
God had led him safely onwards
Into the great unknown,
To a land where blessing followed
And his trust in God had grown.

Genesis 15:5-6

He took him outside and said, "Look up at the sky and count the stars, if indeed you can count them." Then He said to him, "So shall your offspring be." Abram believed the LORD, and He credited it to him as righteousness.

God had showed him lands aplenty
Which his kin would take and own
From Egypt's river to Euphrates –
Foretold promise still to come.
He'd been true when Abram's doubt
Led to sin and to his shame –
Ishmael, not the child of promise;
God alone knew Hagar's pain.

Now Abram had a new name,
And a covenant with God,
For an everlasting possession:
This land in which he trod.
'Abraham' the name he'd carry,
Looked ahead with joy and hope,
Despite advancing earthly years,
Saw the son of whom God spoke,

Saw the future now unfolding,
And blessings yet to be,
A promised city with foundations,
Established through eternity.
He marvelled how such faltering faith
Could bring such full reward;
A city made and ruled by God,
Heaven alone could yet afford.

As he cradled Isaac lovingly
In ageing, weathered hands,
Twelve tribes, as their founder,
He bowed to all God's plans.
When hope seems lost, dreams shattered,
We can trust God's word anew;
He who promised still is faithful,
As he says, thus will He do.

We can trust God's word eternal,
Place our lives into His care,
For the one who flung stars into space
Knows our needs and hears our prayer.
We can trust Him with our future,
With our present and our past,
Looking forward to that city
With foundations that will last.

God's Provision

Isaac the gentle, patient son
Some thought would never be,
Born to aged parents,
God's will his destiny.

He went in meek submission
To die on Mount Moriah,
But in his stead God sent a ram
Caught near rock and briar.

He wed his father's choice of bride,
Rebekah, young and fair,
Accepted as a gift from God,
Prayed for offspring she might bare.

He pleaded for his barren wife
In long and fervent prayer;
God heard his cry and sent twin sons
Who fierce rivalry would share.

Though Isaac sinned when famine struck,
Declared Rebekah as his sibling,
He opened Abraham's wells – long shut –
And this from God brought blessing.

Genesis 25:21

Isaac prayed to the LORD on behalf of his wife, because she was childless. The LORD answered his prayer, and his wife Rebekah became pregnant.

In later years he aimed to bless
Esau his favoured firstborn;
By Jacob's scheming he's denied
Yet his faith is not undone.

This self-effacing servant,
Still faithful to life's ending,
Trusted in God's greater plan,
For the Saviour God was sending.

A Life Transformed

A grasper, a deceiver,
A fighter of his clan;
Such was Jacob's reputation,
What factors shaped this man?
He claimed his brother's birthright
For a bowl of meagre potage;
He claimed the bride of his desire
Despite Laban's cunning plotting.

He wrestled the Lord's angel,
His hip was dislocated;
He claimed new name, new status,
Esau once again outwitted.
With Leah and with Rachel,
And with their concubines,
He bore twelve sons who would become
Twelve tribes by God's design.

Genesis 48:15

The God before whom my fathers Abraham and Isaac walked faithfully, the God who has been my shepherd all my life to this day.

He watched them grow, fight and strive,
A diverse group of brothers;
He wept as fairest Rachel died,
Loved her progeny above all others.
He saw proud Joseph rise to be
A leader amongst men,
Had thought him lost forever,
God reunited them again.

Jacob, the simple herdsman,
He marvelled at it all –
His faith in God rewarded,
He'd responded to God's call.
He'd kept the faith and run the race,
God had changed his heart and soul,
No longer the 'supplanter',
God's love had made him whole.

When Dreams Come True

Joseph pondered on the past,
How life had surely been
More fulfilling and amazing
Than any of his dreams.

As he lay now on his deathbed
Blessing both his sons,
Foreknew the exodus of his people
And suffering still to come,

He recalled how God was faithful
In his life, in many ways,
From his youth, when as a herdsman
He watched flocks as they grazed.

He recalled how dreams had led him
To be sold in slavery,
But also meant deliverance,
When from jail he'd been set free.

Though his brothers had ill-treated him,
Wishing he was dead,
Instead of harm, God had a plan
Bringing good to all instead.

Genesis 50:24-25

Then Joseph said to his brothers, "I am about to die. But God will surely come to your aid and take you up out of this land to the land he promised on oath to Abraham, Isaac and Jacob." And Joseph made the Israelites swear an oath and said, "God will surely come to your aid, and then you must carry my bones up from this place."

This had led him on to Egypt,
Where by Potiphar he was given
Opportunity, yet his scheming wife
Had Joseph sent to Pharaoh's prison.

Joseph's faith was not to fail him,
He would help his fellow man,
A butler saved but baker hanged,
Then Pharaoh's dreams began.

No wise man knew their meaning,
Then the butler did recall,
'Joseph can interpret dreams.'[2]
Freedom beckoned after all.

Seven years of plenty,
With seven years of lean,
Seven fat and thin cows,
The truth of Pharaoh's dream.

Good governance required
To prevent his people perishing;
Prime Minister Joseph proved
His ability needed no embellishing.

In Joseph's time of glory,
His brothers sought him out –
Their lives and future threatened
By famine and by drought.

---

[2] Genesis 41:12

God foreknew in His wisdom
That this time would come,
Reuniting brother with brother,
And father with his son.

Joseph wept, recalled the joy,
When he embraced his father Jacob.
Once lost, now found. Jacob kissed his son.
'I knew that God would save us.'

Restored and reunited,
Each event the Lord decided;
Joseph rested with his fathers,
Each step his God had guided.

A Friend of God

Though raised a prince of Egypt,
Moses chose to save his kin,
Knowing as babe mid bulrushes,
God's love had rescued him.

Proud and trusting human strength,
God calls him to submission;
Near burning bush on holy ground,
He gains a new commission.

To a land of milk and honey
The Israelites are to go,
Long promised to their forefathers;
God tells him it is so.

He's called to go to Pharaoh
To tell him of God's bidding,
But says, 'I'm slow of speech and tongue;[3]
Send someone who is willing.'

God sends Aaron, who will speak,
Tell Pharaoh God's command,
But Pharaoh's heart is hardened.
'Israel's children won't leave this land.'[4]

Hebrews 11:26

[Moses] regarded disgrace for the sake of Christ as of greater value than the treasures of Egypt, because he was looking ahead to his reward.

---

[3] Exodus 4:10
[4] Exodus 5:2

God sends plague, Pharaoh repents;
But his remorse is fleeting,
Until death's angel passes over,
His firstborn son lies dying.

Soon the Exodus begins,
The Israelites reach dry ground;
Pharaoh's men, still in pursuit,
Midst Red Sea all are drowned.

The land of promise beckons them,
The Israelites groan and murmur;
Moses cares and intercedes,
The Lord provides them manna.

Moses, faithful to his Lord,
Through wilderness leads the way,
Guided through each night by fire
And a pillar of cloud each day.

He communes with God on mountain top;
Ten Commandments he receives,
Engraved in stone, rules for life,
For all who will believe.

Because of sin at Rephidim,
Moses won't reach the Promised Land,
But God calls him up Mount Nebo
To view all that God has planned.

And when his time on earth was done,
No human bore him to the grave;
Buried by his God alone,
Enshrined in hearts of those he'd saved.

Yet he would reach the Promised Land
Through the riches of God's grace,
Transfigured with Elijah,
Meeting Jesus face to face.

A man of faith, a friend of God,
Who found strength from above,
Believed all God had promised,
Rewarded by His love.

Faith in His Future

Adele Pilkington

COURAGEOUS FAITH

1 Samuel 2:30

Those who honour me I will honour, but those who despise me will be disdained.

Introduction

The passage in Hebrews chapter 11 only mentions two women specifically by name: Sarah and Rahab. However, it does not take long to identify, in both the Old and New Testaments, many other women whose lives were characterised by great faith in God, often at significant potential costs to themselves. Sarah and Elizabeth both trusted in God's promise that they would bear children, when from a biological perspective this was no longer possible. Rahab and Ruth chose to put their faith in the God of Abraham, Isaac and Jacob, rather than follow the pagan religions with which they had grown up. In both cases their faith brought personal deliverance and also proved to be central to God's plan of sending a Saviour through the tribe of Judah and the lineage of King David.

Hebrews 11:31

By faith the prostitute Rahab, because she welcomed the spies, was not killed with those who were unbelieving.

Deborah was an unusual woman in her time, in that her gifts of wisdom and leadership were acknowledged and she had the role of judge. In a society which did not revere women, she had the courage to speak out in response to God's guidance to her, even when the male leaders around her were reluctant to act. Her courage resulted in the deliverance of her people. Deborah's story also introduces Jael, another courageous woman whose action was essential to God's plan but who, like Rahab and Ruth, had followed other religions before acting faithfully for the one true God.

Women such as Esther and Mary obeyed God's instructions despite risk to their lives and reputations, with their faith bringing a greater reward than they could have imagined. Anna is an example of a woman who never stopped praying for something she knew God had promised. Even though society ignored Anna and her plight, God rewarded her faith in the latter years of her life.

The following verses give a brief insight into the lives of these mostly ordinary women who displayed extraordinary faith in God. There are countless other women through history who have, despite overwhelming odds or societal consequences, placed their trust in the one true and living God who is ever faithful. May their lives and stories be an inspiration for us too!

Hebrews 11:35

Women received back their dead, raised to life again. There were others who were tortured, refusing to be released so that they might gain an even better resurrection.

Lives with Purpose

Perfect peace the prize of faith,
Knowing God is in control,
Safe in His care, amid life's storms,
Finding rest for a weary soul.

Finding doubt and fear have passed
Knowing His Word is His truth,
The joy Mary and Anna shared,
And Deborah, Esther, and Ruth.

Each had lives that brought great trials,
Misunderstood within their time;
They battled hardship, earthly powers,
For a destiny divinely designed.

God loves each one, daughter and son;
Each life his hands have formed;
Each has a purpose to fulfil,
Known by God before they're born.

We can feel our 'little lives'
Are of no consequence
In the wider scheme of things
And the maze of world events.

Philemon 1:6

I pray that your partnership with us in the faith may be effective in deepening your understanding of every good thing we share for the sake of Christ.

The life of each woman of faith
Speaks afresh from Bible pages,
And the God in whom they trusted,
Ever faithful – He never changes.

Hope Fulfilled

How Sarah longed to hold a child
That she could call her own;
She'd watch as Hagar fondly held
Ishmael, her baby son.

She thought of how so long ago
Her husband reassured her
That soon their joy would be complete
As father and as mother.

Sarah wept recalling years
That passed with hope receding –
A barren womb and aching heart,
No child despite her pleading.

Unanswered prayer (or so it seemed)
That God forgot her cry,
And now her ageing body
Reinforced all she'd denied.

Then one day a stranger came
And told her God would send
A child of promise, blessed son;
On this truth she could depend.

Hebrews 11:11

By faith even Sarah, who was past childbearing age, was enabled to bear children because she considered Him faithful who had made the promise.

Adele Pilkington

She laughed, yet hung on every word
The stranger said on parting:
'Is anything too hard for God?'
Inside her new life starting.

She clung on with faith, hope renewed,
Nine months anticipating.
Miraculous blessing! Isaac born!
Joy beyond their expectation!

Nothing too hard, indeed, she thought,
This child, the hope of nations.
Her faith renewed, her heart rejoiced
In the one true God of creation.

A Hidden Promise

A woman of such ill repute,
An outcast of her tribe,
Yet deeds recorded in God's word,
Her name recalled with pride.
Rahab, woman of the night,
Shunned by her kin and nation,
Yet true and faithful to her God,
Determining her salvation.

The tribes of Israel sent forth spies
To Jericho to plunder;
Danger lay within the walls
To tear the spies asunder.
Rahab hid them in her home,
Fearless in her act,
Displayed red cord to signify
Her home wouldn't be attacked.

Hebrews 31:11
*By faith the prostitute Rahab, because she welcomed the spies,
was not killed with those who were disobedient.*

The trumpets sound, and all around
City walls were tumbling;
Safe inside, Rahab and spies;
Jericho's future crumbling.
Her life preserved, she starts afresh,
Salmon's spouse, Boaz her son;
Her saving faith a living proof
God honours those who honour Him.

Faith that Delivers

Deborah pondered as she sat
Underneath the old palm tree
That lay twixt Ramah and Bethel,
What would her solution be?

Deborah's people quaked in fear;
As Jabin and chief Sisera
Threatened to overpower them,
They cried out for a deliverer.

Deborah sought out Barak,
Advised him of God's plan:
He was to head to Tabor's mount
With ten thousand fighting men.

Barak's heart was fearful;
'I'll go if you will come.'
'I'll come,' she said, 'but honour due
Will be given to a woman.'

Sisera and his chariots
Were routed on that day;
He fled to ally Heber's tent
Where only danger lay.

Judges 4:14

Then Deborah said to Barak, "Go! This is the day the LORD has given Sisera into your hands. Has not the LORD gone ahead of you?" So Barak went down Mount Tabor, with ten thousand men following him.

Jael, Heber's wife, said, 'Come inside.'
Thirsty Sisera asked for water.
Drinking in, he failed to see
The hammer meant for slaughter.

Jael drove the tent peg in his head,
Barak pursued his foe;
'Your enemy is dead inside,'
As Deborah did foreknow.

Deborah's voice sang out in praise –
Peace had been restored;
Her people saved, the victory due
To her ever faithful Lord.

Reaping her Reward

'Your people shall be my people,
And your God shall be my God' –
Courage through adversity,
The path that Ruth had trod.

Widowed at an early age,
She chose to leave her kin and land,
Followed mother-in-law Naomi,
Who could not understand;

Embraced the God of Israel,
Her future in His hands.
Whilst Naomi doubts God's goodness
'On His Word,' Ruth said, 'I'll stand.'

Ruth gleaned in harvest fields,
Met kinsman Boaz, kindly owner,
Not knowing that God's plan
For her was Boaz – her redeemer.

Boaz smiles to see Ruth there,
Instructs his men to aid her,
Leaving grain from bundles thick,
Enabling Ruth to gather.

Ruth 1:16

Where you go I will go, and where you stay I will stay. Your people will be my people and your God my God.

Ruth tells of Boaz' kindness;
Naomi, seeing God's direction,
Praises God and tells Ruth,
'Claim the right of your redemption.'

Ruth lies at Boaz' feet.
'Take your cloak and spread it here,'
Boaz gently tells her,
Gave Ruth grain, she knew no fear.

He buys Naomi's inheritance,
Thus gaining Ruth as bride.
His kinfolk give their blessing;
God's will is satisfied.

Ruth, faithfulness rewarded,
Bears Obed, precious one,
Ancestor of King David
And Jesus, God's own son.

For Such a Time

'For such a time as this…'
Those words rang in her ears
As Esther knelt before the king;
God melted all her fears.

Her life hung in the balance,
Haman's wish that she might die;
This fate befell Queen Vashti
And waited Mordecai.

She thought fondly of her uncle,
The sacrifice he'd made,
Enabling her to be a Queen,
This graceful Jewish handmaid.

She thought of Haman's evil plan
To see her uncle on the gallows
For refusing to bow down to one
So prideful and so shallow.

Her faith in God brought hope and peace;
There was another way
To save him and her people too,
So silently she prayed.

Esther 4:14

For if you remain silent at this time, relief and deliverance for the Jews will arise from another place, but you and your father's family will perish. And who knows but that you have come to your royal position for such a time as this?

The king – no longer angry –
Half his kingdom he would give;
She had only to make her wish.
What to ask, that all might live?

A banquet, then a second one,
The King and Haman present.
Haman's pride was multiplied.
The king nodded his consent.

That night the king in fitful sleep
Read the records of his reign;
Amid the pages, Mordecai –
A hero deserving fame.

The records showed that Mordecai
Had foiled an evil plan.
What honour had been bestowed
On such a worthy man?

No honour sought, his only aim
Had been unto that day
To do his duty, serve his King;
Yet Haman sought to slay.

The king consults his minister.
'Haman, what are we to do
To reward one who delights the king,
And give him honour due?'

'Who else but me can be that man?'
Haman did surmise,
'He should wear royal robes and ride a steed,
That all might see his prize.'

The king instructs Haman in his role:
'As you say, so let it be;
Give Mordecai this honour due
And do the deed for me.'

Haman obeys with heavy heart,
Looks forward to the banquet,
But the king learns of his evil plan
To kill this faithful servant.

The king enraged, the gallows wait,
True justice to Haman afforded;
Her people and her uncle saved,
Queen Esther's faith rewarded.

The Lord's Handmaiden

Before the angel's visit
Her life was ordinary:
Betrothal to a carpenter;
Mary, eager soon to marry.

'How can it be?' she wondered,
As lowly virgin maiden,
That she should bear a son,
Be the one that God had chosen.

The angel said, 'The Holy Spirit's power
By grace will overcome;
The babe that you will carry
Is Jesus, God's own Son.'

Such blessing for her people,
God's act of mercy and grace,
The Messiah so long promised,
A Saviour from her race.

'As handmaiden of my Lord,
Be it to me as you have said.'
Yet mindful of Joseph her betrothed,
Her joy was mixed with dread.

Luke 1:38

*"I am the Lord's servant," Mary answered. "May your word
to me be fulfilled." Then the angel left her.*

But through dream an angel told him,
'Fear not to marry Mary.
This act is done by God Most High;
Jesus, the Son she'll carry.'

Joseph and Mary, joined by faith,
Believed all God foretold;
Mid stable dark, in manger bare,
Saw incense, myrrh and gold.

A host of angels, shining star,
Shepherds through the night,
Three kings who travelled from afar
Create a wondrous sight.

Their tiny babe they bowed before,
The Lord of highest heaven;
Yet gifted to their loving care,
By faith they'd do God's bidding.

Faithfulness Rewarded

What joy had filled her soul
The day that Mary came!
'The mother of my Lord,'
She called out Mary's name.

The child within her womb,
Waited for so long,
Leapt with joy as Mary too
Rejoiced with her in song.

Elizabeth already knew
The fruit of her womb was blessed,
But Mary's babe was God's own Son;
They wept as they caressed.

No longer doubt in Mary's mind,
The news of the angel confirmed,
Her cousin's babe, also a miracle,
After barren years, her faith undeterred.

Whilst Elizabeth was filled with joy,
Her husband could not believe
The news the angel brought to him,
That his aged wife had conceived.

Luke 1: 24-25

Elizabeth became pregnant and for five months remained in seclusion. "The Lord has done this for me," she said. "In these days He has shown His favour and taken away my disgrace among the people."

Filled with the Spirit from his mother's womb,
Turning his people to their God,
A nomadic life would be his lot,
Preparing the way for his Lord.

For disbelief, Zacharias wouldn't speak
Until his son was born,
Yet on that day he would indicate,
'Yes, his name is John.'

Elizabeth recalled, as her son grew,
The message the angel had given –
'Repent and believe; be baptised.' –
Many finding their sins forgiven.

Given for a purpose, destined to be
The one to prepare the way,
His to decrease as Christ would increase,
Mission ending swiftly one day.

The cruellest fate, the price of a dance,
Herodias outwitting the king;
Salome smiled, the king so beguiled,
The head of the Baptist his offering.

Yet Elizabeth's faith had found its reward;
Her son had been faithful and true.
Reunited together in heaven they'd share
The riches their faith had accrued.

Adele Pilkington

Answered Prayer

As she watched with eager eyes
The tiny form before her,
Joy filled her aching soul afresh –
This babe, her Lord and Saviour.

Long hard years had Anna spent,
A widow, poor, alone,
Longing for this child to come,
Messiah, Holy One.

Each year spent in fervent prayer
Seemed only but a day;
God's grace, her faith united;
Her sorrows washed away.

Widowed at an early age,
No child to call her own,
No support in later years,
God's temple was her home.

Eagerly she reached the crowds.
Good News was hers to tell,
So others might share in her joy,
Worship the babe – Immanuel.

Luke 2:38

Coming up to them at that very moment, she gave thanks to God and spoke about the child to all who were looking forward to the redemption of Jerusalem.

Faith in His Future

Adele Pilkington

GROWING FAITH

1 Thessalonians 1:3

We remember before our God and Father your work produced by faith, your labour prompted by love, and your endurance inspired by hope in our Lord Jesus Christ.

Introduction

God's word can and does teach us much about faith. However, we can only really begin to experience the reality of faith in God, as described in the lives of the Bible characters highlighted on these pages, by putting our faith into action. The Bible tells us that we can have faith as tiny as a mustard seed and yet be able to achieve great things. It is not the size of our faith but the person in whom we place our faith that determines the outcome.

Matthew 17:20 (NIV)
[Jesus] replied, "Because you have so little faith. Truly I tell you, if you have faith as small as a mustard seed, you can say to this mountain, 'Move from here to there,' and it will move. Nothing will be impossible for you."

When we place our faith in Christ, who has overcome all of the powers or forces that can ever cause us to fear or threaten our security, we can be sure that our faith will be sufficient.

The more we are able to exercise this faith, the more we find that we can trust in God for even more challenging events. This does not mean that the very foundations of our lives will not be shaken, but God will see us safely through to our eternal home. Each of us has a different journey of life, with different life circumstances, but in all things we will find God faithful if we place our trust in Him. The following section explores that journey of personal faith and reflects on the eternal security we have in Christ.

Philippians 1:21
For to me, to live is Christ and to die is gain.

Faith with Foundations

'Forsaking all I trust in Him' –
Easy words to say,
But when troubles come, or fears assail,
Do we doubt or do we pray?

Do we find our strength in Christ alone,
In the power of His salvation,
Or do we trust ourselves, our wit or guile?
It can only bring frustration.

Christ's atoning blood, His sacrifice,
This one way alone can span
The gulf between a holy God
And finite, sinful man.

Faith established in His power,
In Christ our hope, can't waver;
Salvation in no other name,
His finished work has met God's favour.

1 Peter 1:5

You who through faith are shielded by God's power until the coming of the salvation that is ready to be revealed in the last time.

God Cares

When the world turns away,
When there's fear in your heart,
God cares.

When you're helpless and hopeless,
If guilt tears you apart,
God cares.

When the things you have worked for are dust,
When you're lacking in faith, and it's so hard to trust,
God cares.

When the darkness brings dread and you can't see the light,
Thoughts cloud with confusion, no strength for the fight,
God cares.

When you're lonely and tearful, in need of a friend,
When your problems are mounting, you can't see the end,
God cares.

---

1 Peter 5:7

Cast all your anxiety on Him because He cares for you.

Adele Pilkington

Is it only in trouble, when resources are few
That we cry out, 'Oh God, how I need you'?
God longs to be with us in joy and in sorrows,
Guiding todays and planning tomorrows;
Our burdens are lifted, our struggle is gone,
We have strength to continue and hope to go on,
Because God cares.

One Way

God's Word is life, and all will find
Within the pages peace of mind
For all who love and trust the Lord,
Life's questions answered in His Word.
Each verse will draw us near to Him,
Enlightened hearts rejoice within,
To understand his Master plan,
His boundless love before life began.

But the Word of God is very clear:
Only one way can draw us near,
One Way, one Truth, one God above,
Who died and saved us by His love.
No other road can lead to Him,
No other means to save from sin.
Christ is the Way, the Truth, the Life;
No man-made effort can suffice.
Without this simple trust and faith,
Our hope is lost, our work is waste.

John 14:6

*Jesus answered, "I am the way and the truth and the life. No
one comes to the Father except through me."*

No idol, relic, man-made god
Can offer what our Lord's secured.
Only in Christ can we be whole.
Only He can change the sinner's soul
By repentance, faith and trust in Christ;
Renewed, redeemed by His sacrifice;
New life, new Spirit, God within,
To live forever and reign with Him.

The Bride of Christ

One husband for life and for each man one wife
Is God's heavenly plan and His call,
That together we'd grow and by His love would show
The love that Christ has for us all.

God's desire from the first was to dwell here on earth,
To fellowship, share in our gladness;
But sin came and stopped Him, our God turned away,
His heart filled with grief and with sadness.

And so for God's plan, the redemption of man,
That fellowship might be restored,
Christ's death on the cross, so great was the cost,
To deal with the sin He abhorred.

Now each who receive Him will find God is love –
This fellowship cannot be earned –
For we are His Church, His people, His Bride
For whom one day our Lord will return.

He will take us that day to a heavenly home –
A Bridegroom awaiting His Bride –
So we must be ready, be pure and prepared,
Without sin or envy or pride.

Revelation 21:2

I saw the Holy City, the new Jerusalem, coming down out of heaven from God, prepared as a bride beautifully dressed for her husband.

By living our lives as Christ meant us to live,
By following close to His Word,
Our union on earth will be blessed from above,
Our union in heaven secured.

Selfless Love

'Love one another as I have loved you.'
This is the truth that He taught.
In service to others, our family and friends,
There is strength in the message Christ brought.

That our lives might reflect the love that is Christ
So that all who see us might know
That our service is merely a token to Him
For the great debt of thanks that we owe.

To love one another is easy when those
Whom we love will love us in return,
But to love those who hate you, or taunt you and jeer,
Is a lesson that's so hard to learn.

And yet, Christ's example is there for us all,
Through His life to His death on the cross;
No matter the costs to ourselves or our own,
We must never consider it loss.

For by following Christ in the way that He leads,
We can know that our future's secure,
And our service is gaining a greater reward
Than this world can ever ensure.

---

1 John 4:10

*This is love: not that we loved God, but that He loved us and
sent His Son as an atoning sacrifice for our sins.*

Adele Pilkington

Sacrifice

No greater love could ever be
Than He who gave his life for me.
No greater gift was ever given
Than our Lord sent to earth from heaven,
To show us in His daily way
How to love and how to pray,
How to serve and how to give,
And live as we were meant to live.
And through His suffering and pain
Our hearts are cleansed, we're born again.
But we must look upon that tree
And see what we were meant to see:
An empty cross; our Saviour's risen;
He lives and reigns, our Lord in heaven.

1 John 3:1

See what great love the Father has lavished on us, that we should be called children of God! And that is what we are!

Living Waters

As cleansing waters o'er me roll,
Wash all my sins away,
My life I give to Jesus;
My soul is His today.
Life-giving blood of Jesus
Was shed in love for me,
And now I long to follow Him,
Whose love has set me free.
I'll follow Him through darkness,
Along the narrow road.
I'll follow him; the power of death
No longer has a hold.
I consecrate my life to Him.
Lord, on you I can depend –
Your love sustaining through my life
Until the journey's end.

Mark 16:16

Whoever believes and is baptized will be saved, but whoever does not believe will be condemned.

Adele Pilkington

No Better Friend

I've got the best friend anyone could know;
He's always there to listen, no matter where I go;
He doesn't talk to others about the things I've said;
He'll never turn and run from me when trouble rears its head.
He's there in your life if you want Him to be;
Jesus loves helping others – it's His way, you see –
And He will live in your life if you want it that way;
All you need do is just kneel and pray.

John 15:15

I no longer call you servants, because a servant does not know his master's business. Instead, I have called you friends, for everything that I learned from my Father I have made known to you.

All the Days of My Life

Lord Jesus, the Shepherd who cares,
All the days of my life you will share
Your infinite love and your grace.

Lord Jesus, the Shepherd who died,
All the days you are there by my side,
Guarding and guiding my way.

Lord Jesus, my Servant and King,
All the days may my heart gladly sing
Songs of thanksgiving and praise

For Jesus, who bore sin and shame
That my life might be saved by His name,
To live and to walk in His way –
A redeemed child of God, born again.

Lord Jesus, the Shepherd who cares,
All the days of my life, till their end,
May I reach other souls by your grace,
Risen King, till you come once again.

Psalm 23:1-3

The LORD is my shepherd, I lack nothing. He makes me lie down in green pastures, He leads me beside quiet waters, He refreshes my soul.

Adele Pilkington

Gratitude

Where would I be without Jesus?
What would I do without Him?
Life would seem futile, so pointless,
The future uncertain and grim.

My life would have no direction;
My soul would not sing for joy,
For my Saviour and Father in heaven
And their love which no man can destroy.

For with God and with Jesus beside me,
I know I have nothing to fear;
For whatever troubles beset me,
A hand of protection is near.

And no matter how rocky the road seems,
The future will always be bright,
As death is no longer an ending
But the road to His kingdom of light,

Where once again we will meet loved ones
Who left us along life's way,
Where pain and all suffering has ended
And we'll enjoy His presence always.

John 15:13
Greater love has no one than this: to lay down one's life for one's friends.

So where would I be without Jesus?
I'll tell you what He means to me:
Faith that's secure, love that's assured
From now through eternity.

Adele Pilkington

Enduring Faith

Without faith we cannot please
The God who loves us dearly;
We must believe He is who He says,
Give our lives in service freely.

For by our faith we signify
We know what can't be seen;
Our God is King of all the earth,
Of all created things.

By our faith we do proclaim
We know that on that day
When Christ returns, all knees will bow
And magnify His name.

We know we have a hope that's sure –
Not in human power or wisdom,
But in the one unchanging God,
His eternal coming Kingdom.

Let's hold on to faith that's true,
Ensure His will is done,
As sons and daughters of the King
Until His Kingdom comes.

Hebrews 11:6

And without faith it is impossible to please God, because anyone who comes to Him must believe that He exists and that He rewards those who earnestly seek Him.

Faith in His Future

Epilogue

Placing our faith in Christ is something which is not without risk. God may often call us to undertake tasks which are well outside our comfort zone, or involve entering situations where there might be threat to our personal safety or that of loved ones. Thus far in the Western world we have been fortunate in enjoying relative freedom of expression in relation to our faith. This freedom is now in danger in our own lands, due to the forces of secular humanism within society, and is something we need to protect at all costs. It is certainly something which is not guaranteed for many in others lands, where even to name Christ's name or to profess allegiance to Him can result in persecution, suffering and even death.

There are many Christians who would rather face this risk than deny their Saviour and Lord. However, the consequences may be considerable for both them and their families. Fortunately there are a number of charities that support the persecuted church around the world and provide practical help, spiritual support and encouragement for those who face such hardships. This help can be essential to enable those who are persecuted because of their faith in Christ to stand firm.

In this regard, it is intended that 100% of the royalties received by the author from the sale of this book will be distributed by her evenly among the following charities:

- Barnabas Fund
  www.barnabasfund.org/uk/
- Humanitarian Aid Relief Trust (HART)
  www.hart-uk.org
- Release International
  www.releaseinternational.org

Matthew 25:40
The King will reply, 'Truly I tell you, whatever you did for one of the least of these brothers and sisters of mine, you did for me.'

Index